TESS WHITEHURST
ARTWORK BY TAMMY WAMPLER

The Wild Witch Oracle

SHAPESHIFTERS, REBELS & QUEENS

THE WILD WITCH ORACLE
Shapeshifters, Rebels & Queens

Copyright © 2025 Tess Whitehurst
Artwork Copyright © 2025 Tammy Wampler

All rights reserved. Other than for personal use, no part of these cards or this book may be reproduced in any way, in whole or part, without the written consent of the copyright holder or publisher. This publication is intended for spiritual and emotional guidance only. The content is not intended to replace medical assistance or treatment. The views and opinions expressed by the author, both within and outside of this publication, do not necessarily reflect the views of the publisher.

Published by Blue Angel Publishing®
10 Trafford Court, Wheelers Hill,
Victoria, Australia 3150
E-mail: info@blueangelonline.com
Website: www.blueangelonline.com

Editors: Cherise Asmah and Jules Sutherland

Blue Angel is a registered trademark of Blue Angel Gallery Pty Ltd.

ISBN: 978-1-922574-39-8

Printed on sustainably sourced paper,
with soy-based ink.

Contents

YOUR WILDNESS BECKONS 7
How to Prepare Your Deck for Use 11
How to do a Reading with *The Wild Witch Oracle* 12

THE CARDS
1. BLODEUWEDD 20
2. ALDER WITCH 23
3. MELISSA 26
4. AMBERELLA 29
5. VIRGO PRIESTESS 32
6. THETIS 35
7. ANNE BOLEYN 38
8. CAPRICORN PRIESTESS 41
9. OSHUN 44
10. CLIODHNA 47
11. ELEANOR OF AQUITAINE 50
12. ETAIN 53
13. LI BAN 56
14. ARADIA 59
15. LIBRA PRIESTESS 62
16. MINERVA 65
17. HESPERA 68
18. ALKONOST 71

19. REDWOOD QUEEN 74
20. MAEVE 77
21. CIRCE 80
22. ANGELICA 83
23. QUEEN MAB 86
24. SCORPIO PRIESTESS 89
25. MORGAN LE FAY 92
26. SAMOVILA 95
27. OAK QUEEN 98
28. SINANN 101
29. ARIANRHOD 104
30. STELLA MARIS 107
31. EAGLE PRIESTESS 110
32. CAER IBORMEITH 113
33. QUEEN VICTORIA 116
34. BLACK ANNIS 119
35. ARIES PRIESTESS 122
36. ASPEN PRINCESS 125
37. MELUSINE 128
38. VERDANDI 131
39. FREYA 134
40. ELIZABETH WOODVILLE 137
41. ANGRBODA 140
42. MARY, QUEEN OF SCOTS 143
43. OSTARA 146
44. ISIS 149

About the Author 153
About the Artist 155

Your Wildness Beckons

Your natural state is one of liberation, inspiration, and incredible power. You are a creature of the elements and the earth, most at home with the fire of the sun enlivening you, a vision of glimmering water replenishing your spirit, your bare feet on the fertile soil, and the wind blowing through your hair.

The feminine spirits of this deck—the queens, shapeshifters, and rebels—are here to call you back to your native wildness: to remind you that you are wise, independent, empowered, and free.

No one owns you. Nothing limits you. Your choices and your authority are your own. You are a divine child and a priestess of the Goddess. A current of primordial power runs through you: you can channel it for healing, transformation, and manifesting the truest and most authentic desires of your heart.

Some of the cards in this deck depict goddesses from world religions. You will discover that their stories often unfold for us differently here than they have in the past. In other words, in the present moment and through the context of this oracle deck, the goddesses reveal more of their secrets and bring more of their mysteries to light. The rise of the Great Goddess, the upswing of the feminine principle, and the living spark in each glorious work of art alchemically interweave, allowing us to perceive and understand these ancient myths with greater lucidity and depth.

Queens and other distinguished leaders—now in the spirit realm but who once walked the earth—also appear in this deck. While many or most of these historical figures would probably not have identified themselves as witches, they are distinguished by the authority they wielded in life along with their mastery of transforming and manifesting conditions in accordance with their will. Invariably, they are women who made their own rules and refused to shrink themselves to fit into restrictive cultural paradigms. In some cases, the acute injustices they faced allow them to confer a unique wisdom to us now that they are on the other side.

You will also encounter faeries, astrological priestesses, and forces of nature. They, too, swirl their currents of primordial and archetypal wisdom into the mix.

All the feminine divinities and ascended masters in this deck are here to call you back to your independence and remind you of your power. Your wildness, your magic, and your radiant beauty are already right here, within you. The time to awaken to them is now.

HOW TO PREPARE YOUR DECK FOR USE

You can begin using your deck for readings and inspiration right away, but you will enhance your connection with the oracle and amplify its accuracy and potency if you perform this simple blessing and activation ritual first.

Take your deck outside, preferably somewhere secluded where you won't be disturbed. This could be a forest, a desert, the edge of a moving body of water, a city park, or even your own balcony, deck, or backyard. Anywhere that feels right will do, at any point in the moon cycle and at any time of day, as long as it's in the fresh air and under the sky.

Remove the cards from the box and give them an initial shuffle. Sit or stand comfortably and hold the cards in your open palms, as if you are offering them up to the sky. Say:

Great Goddess, I invoke you.
Great Goddess, I honor you.
Thank you for filling these cards with your intelligence,
your authority, and your living spirit.

Imagine, feel, and sense a beautiful light filling your deck.

Now, sandwich the deck between your palms, so you are holding your hands in prayer pose. Move your hands so the sides of your thumbs are touching your heart area. Close your eyes and say:

*Great Goddess, thank you for awakening my independence, magic, and wildness.
Thank you for opening my heart to the wisdom of this deck, and for aligning me with the powerful divinities, queens, and nature spirits herein.*

Feel and sense the light in your heart merging with the light of the deck. Say:

*Thank you, thank you, thank you. Blessed be.
And so it is.*

HOW TO DO A READING WITH *THE WILD WITCH ORACLE*

If you wish, you can light a candle, or go outside under the open sky. But you can also do a reading anytime, anywhere, provided you have enough quiet time to breathe, relax, and focus your mind.

Hold the deck in both hands. Close your eyes. Take a few deep breaths and then allow your breathing to be natural as you continue to relax your body and mind. When you feel calm and grounded, inwardly ask your question, or bring your current challenge to mind. You can also perform a general reading to receive guidance for the day, week, or month ahead.

Phrase your inquiry in an open-ended way. Instead of asking a yes-or-no question, like, "Should I apply for this job?" or, "Is this relationship right for me?" you might silently say something like, "Thank you for giving me insight into this job opportunity," or, "What do I need to know about this relationship?"

If you're interested in gaining insight into a particular situation, bring the situation to mind and say or think something like, "Thank you for showing me the wisdom that will serve me best."

If you're doing a general reading for the day, week, or month ahead, you could think, "Thank you for revealing the divine wisdom that will most help me today (or this week, or this month)."

For an even more general reading, you could simply just say or think, "Thank you for showing me what I need to know."

Shuffle the cards in any way you like, for as long as you like. (Don't worry about when to stop shuffling. Whenever you stop will be the right time.) Then, draw one, three, or four cards from the top of the deck, depending on the card spread you choose.

For a one-card reading, simply remove the top card from the deck and place it in front of you, facing up. Gaze at the image. Soak in its beauty and receive its energetic essence. Intuitively and wordlessly allow yourself to sense its message. Then, look up the accompanying description in this guidebook. Allow the guidance to wash over you, and be alert to any phrases that particularly stand out as you read.

For a three-card reading, remove the top three cards from the deck, and spread them out, face up, left to right.

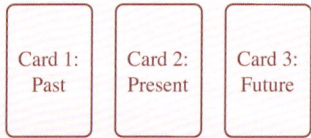

Card One provides insight into the past, and/or the roots of the challenge, issue, or situation.
Card Two offers guidance with regard to the present.
Card Three is your advice about moving forward and may provide clarity about what to expect.

First, gaze at the images for a moment and enjoy their beauty. Then, look them up, one by one, in this book. Allow yourself to sense and know how each card's wisdom applies to you now.

For a four-card reading, sit facing east. After shuffling, arrange the cards in a diamond shape, placing Card One at the top of the spread, Card Two to the right, Card Three at the bottom, and Card Four to the left.

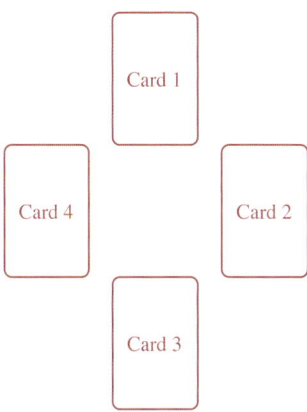

Card One is in the air position. It offers guidance about your thoughts and ideas: how to contemplate your situation and how you can use your mental powers to the fullest.

Card Two is in the fire position: it tells you about your passions and how the situation can foster transformation and dynamic change.

Card Three is in the water position: it offers insight into your emotions, memories, and dreams.

Card Four is in the earth position: how can you get more grounded and take concrete steps in the physical world that will both support you and bring the most benefits to all concerned?

Remember: always gaze at the images and enjoy their beauty for a moment before you look them up in this book. This will help you receive the wisdom in a deeper, more complete, and more nuanced way.

The Cards

1. Blodeuwedd

BE TRUE TO YOURSELF

•

Release your need to please. Refuse the roles that have been appointed to you externally and without your consent. Discover and express essential personal truths.

•

LEAVE SITUATIONS THAT ARE NOT RIGHT FOR you or be willing to dismantle them utterly as you follow the stirrings of your heart.

Blodeuwedd, whose name means "flower-faced," is a Welsh goddess who symbolizes the sacred land in full bloom. She was formed from blossoms and flower spirits to serve as the queen and consort of the Welsh hero of divine parentage, Lleu Llaw Gyffes.

But it turned out Blodeuwedd did not want to marry Lleu Llaw Gyffes. As punishment for rebelling against the destiny for which she was created, she was transformed into an owl.

What is it that you think you must do, but that you don't want to do? What cultural tradition does not resonate with your authentic self?

In her transformation into an owl, Blodeuwedd discovers she can fly, see in the dark, shapeshift into other forms, and look deeply into the heart of all beings and situations.

You, too, will be rewarded when you act on your own behalf and refuse to go along with the plan others have laid out for you.

If Blodeuwedd had denied her feelings and impulses, she may have lived as a queen, but a queen with her powers gravely restricted: a queen who could only express a small fraction of her truest, wisest, most passionate and magical self.

Recognize where you have internalized limiting expectations and beliefs about who you should be, how you should look, or what you should do with your precious time on Earth.

You must not perpetuate the status quo or stay on the surface of things. Express your needs. State your boundaries. Take audacious and outrageous action and let go of what you no longer want.

When you do so, that which is in alignment with your destiny will stay. That which is not will either dissolve away or transform into something else. And you will clear the way for your most ideal life to unfold.

2. Alder Witch

TEND TO YOUR WELLNESS AND EMOTIONS

•

Honor your emotions while also tending to the habits, structures, and paradigms that facilitate your well-being. Tune in and take care. Take the practical steps that will support your inner healing.

•

ALDER IS A TREE OF BOTH WARRIORS AND THE fae: the elements of earth and water. It interweaves the grounded, physical realms of body, habits, and home with your fluid and spiraling depths.

Water without boundaries is a flood. Earth without moisture is a wasteland. When earth and water mutually support each other, healing happens and clarity dawns.

First, get clear on how you are feeling. If one of your feelings is confusion, what, exactly, are you confused about? What is it that you don't quite know, but would like to know? What questions need answering for you to feel some semblance of peace? What feelings have you been ignoring, or failing to notice? Free writing your thoughts and feelings in a journal or notebook will help you sort things out.

While you may not have all the answers, just taking some time to tune in to yourself in this way will provide you with a substantial measure of peace.

Once this step in your self-exploration feels complete, look at what you've written, and ask, "What forms of self-care will best support me at this time?"

First, make a list of basic, physical-world conditions that will nourish you, such as a clean house, a gentle stretch, and a healthy meal. We often can't see all the steps to take with regard to a particular problem or challenge, but it's usually true that you'll feel better and have more of a sense of direction after you clear your clutter or nourish your body with delicious food.

Next, list emotional, energetic steps to self-support, such as meditation, deep breathing, speaking with a therapist, or getting an energy healing. It's okay if not all of them are feasible for you right now. Just look deeply and catalogue the forms of emotional and energetic support that might be beneficial to you at this time.

Now, take a good look at both lists. What's one thing you can do from the first list? What's one thing you can do from the second? Patiently, steadily, and compassionately take one of these loving actions. And then the other. When those are complete, see what unfolds, or perhaps initiate another list item. Don't rush this process. Be patient and systematic as you care for your whole self. In perfect timing, you will experience the healing clarity you seek.

3. Melissa

AWAKEN TO SWEETNESS

•

Open your eyes to a new day and taste the sweetness of life. Release attachment to the past and surrender worry about the future. Be born anew in the present — fully awake and alive.

•

THE PRIMORDIAL MOTHER GODDESS WAS associated with bees in Greek, Roman, and Minoan cultures. She is the Great Mother Bee: she around whom culture is formed, feminine spirit of the earth, wise matriarch, and bestower of sweetness, sustenance, and golden wealth. The Great Bee Goddess also appears as the Greek bee nymph, Melissa (which means honeybee), who shares her name with the priestesses of the Eleusinian Mysteries and the Oracle of Delphi, the Melissae.

In addition to the bee, the butterfly appears with Melissa as a symbol of transformation, and the morning glory as a reminder to reawaken to the endlessly inspiring mystery at the heart of existence.

No matter how many challenges and traumas you've been through in the past, and no matter what mists appear to cloud your future path, you have the present-moment ability to reinvent yourself, draw prosperity into your life, and rediscover the power that's been with you all along.

The most powerful leaders in the land consulted the Melissae (the priestesses of the Oracle of Delphi) at vital moments for advice on how to proceed. Similarly, the wisdom and guidance you need are here for you. Gaze at the bee goddess on the card. Sense her wise clarity and bright inner knowing. Close your eyes, breathe, and feel this wisdom within yourself.

Right this very moment—now—what truth is there for you? What can you let go of, and what is it time for you to embrace? Call up a sense that you are already living your best and most beautiful future. What choices did you make in the present moment, in order to get from here to there?

When you allow your clear and optimistic inner knowing to surface, you can move forward with greater ease than you previously imagined. The Goddess will be with you every step of the way.

4. Amberella

HEAL OLD PATTERNS

•

Romantic love and familial love are interwoven. Just as each can nourish the other, each can also pose a challenge to the other. Pay attention to old family patterns and take steps to heal painful relationship dynamics.

•

AMBERELLA IS A BALTIC SPIRIT WHO BEGAN AS an earthly or divine princess who fell in love with the prince of the sea. When she married him, she left her family and, in time, began to miss them dearly. Instead of allowing Amberella to visit them, the sea prince brought her closer to the shore but held her back from exiting the sea. Unable to speak to her family or stand with them on solid ground, she still wanted to express her love, so she sent pieces of amber as gifts to them in the waves.

In this card image, Amberella has reclaimed her freedom and stepped into even more power than before, triumphantly emerging from the waves with wings made of amber on her back.

If you are currently in a romantic relationship, what issues or challenges mirror past experiences with your family of origin? Even when we go out of our way to select a partner who seems diametrically different from one or more of our childhood guardians, our partner may end up presenting us with many of the same issues we experienced when we were kids.

Whether you're in a romantic relationship or not, take a good look at any unhealed pain or trauma related to your family of origin and your primary caregivers growing up. Even ancestral patterns can be important to look at now: things that may have happened decades and even centuries before you were born. Even though such things are not in any way your fault, they will continue to affect you if you do not get conscious about them and make the deliberate choice to move forward in healthy, new ways.

As you move through these inner explorations and seek to heal and restructure your mental and emotional landscapes, you may want to obtain a lovely piece of amber to carry or wear, as amber is the pure essence of Amberella's love. Every drop of amber holds her wisdom and will support you in enforcing your boundaries, speaking your truth, and rising above the pain of the past.

5. Virgo Priestess

ESTABLISH ORDER

•

Establish greater order, harmony, and wellness in your inner and outer worlds. Change what you can and let go of what you can't. Inhabit your body and settle your anxious mind.

•

VIRGO IS AN EARTH SIGN: PRACTICAL, SENSUAL, and grounded. The Virgo Priestess knows she can calm her anxiety, settle her frenetic energy, and effect lasting positive change by taking concrete action in the physical realm.

It seems you are fretting or worrying about something that is beyond the scope of your influence. The Virgo Priestess guides you to acknowledge what you can't control, but also to recognize what you can. You always have jurisdiction, for example, over your own home. You can't do much to affect the weather, the stock market, or the actions or opinions of others. But you *can* dust your shelves, vacuum your floor, and water your plants. You can't change the genes you were born with, but you can exercise, drink lots of water, and get plenty of sleep.

So often, the inner workings of magic dwell not in spectacular, awe-inspiring acts, but in the seemingly mundane details of life. If you want to be radiantly healthy, or build a remarkable career, or manifest positive change in any life area, it's all about the little things. Over time, particularly when performed with intention, the little things are not actually little. A clean house, an organized desk, a body nourished with fresh air and wholesome food: day in and day out, such things can add up to holistic well-being and triumphant success.

Look honestly at your environment and habits and you will know just what this card is counseling you to do. It may be time to clear clutter, start a new exercise regimen, engage in herbal healing practices, or rearrange your desk. Even if it seems like these topics have nothing to do with your current situation and the object of your inquiry, they very much do. One humble pebble dropped in the lake of your life can bring about a ripple effect of vast, all-encompassing positive change.

Your habits define your trajectory: when you correct your course and stick to it for the long term, you will find yourself in a far different, far better place.

Love yourself. Take care of yourself. Tend to the everyday business of living and set yourself up to comprehensively flourish and thrive.

6. Thetis

CLAIM ABSOLUTE AUTHORITY

•

Let no one limit, capture, or tame you. Claim your authority. Honor your desires, be decisive, and let go of worries about what will happen or what others may think.

•

YOUR AUTHORITY IS VAST AND YOUR ABILITY TO craft your world is all-encompassing.

The sea nymph Thetis appears in Greek mythology as a mother and foster mother of iconic heroes and gods, such as Achilles, Hephaestus, and Dionysus. But in even more ancient times, she may have been honored as the Great Mother Goddess, spirit of the sea, and absolute creator of all.

The two most powerful gods of their day, Zeus and Poseidon, were both in love with Thetis. But at the same time, Zeus feared her and married her off to his mortal grandson in an effort to limit her power. And yet, as the Divine Creatrix, she foresaw even this — even Zeus could not foil her grand design.

Similarly, even if they appear to, no one else holds power over you. You are the boss of your own life, and you always have the right and responsibility to say yes, no, or maybe. You are not beholden to anyone. All your relationships and life conditions are choices you have made, and they are also choices you can unmake.

Like Thetis, when you own your power utterly, you need not broadcast it unless you choose to. You can simply wield it — quietly and without fanfare. You can discreetly swim away, shapeshift into something else, or find your joy in your own unique and personal way. As the undisputed ruler of your own experience, you have nothing to prove to anyone. Your only responsibility is to yourself.

Be utterly clear about who you are, what feels right to you, and what you want. Know down to your deepest depths that you are the queen of your world. Then, act now, act later, or wait until you sense the time is right.

When you honor your inherent freedom and absolute authority, everything will naturally unfold and fall into place.

7. Anne Boleyn

REFUSE TO BE CONTROLLED

•

Set clear boundaries. Refuse to be controlled. Remove yourself from any relationship, job, or living situation in which you are being used, abused, or otherwise mistreated.

•

THE TAPESTRY OF DESTINY IS INTERWOVEN WITH both grave darkness and glorious light. Every life will contain beauty and blessings, along with—at times—unfair treatment and excruciating emotional pain.

If you are currently experiencing any form of suffering or pain, this should not be a source of shame or a reason to berate, blame, or isolate yourself. No one is an island and there is no life into which the cheerful light of the sun unendingly shines.

Queen Anne Boleyn gave birth to Princess Elizabeth I, who grew up to be Queen of England, bringing decades of unprecedented stability and creative rebirth in her royal wake. But long before, Anne Boleyn was horrifically executed at the order of her very own husband while Elizabeth was still a toddler and she herself was in her prime.

The good news is that, unlike Anne Boleyn, there is no relationship you are lawfully or politically bound to stick around for. While it's true that every life contains moments of mistreatment, you don't owe it to anyone to continue to subject yourself to any form of oppression, exploitation, or abuse.

Your authority is intrinsic and all-conquering. You can say no to anything and anyone, at any time, no matter what. Even if there is no controlling or abusive behavior present that you can see, there are no prerequisites to your autonomy. You don't need to prove or explain your decisions to anyone. If you want to go, you can go. If you want to stay, you can stay. And if you want to stay long enough to see if you can successfully enforce a new dynamic or a new set of rules, you absolutely can do that too.

First, allow yourself to know what you want, what you don't want, and what you will and won't accept. Remember that you indeed get to set those conditions and boundaries. Ask the Goddess for guidance and support. And then, with great wisdom and clarity, proceed.

8. Capricorn Priestess

GET TO WORK

●

Work, work, work — with exquisite and unwavering focus. Take one step toward your goal, and then another, with a steady, methodical rhythm. Get to work and you will certainly succeed.

●

THE CAPRICORN PRIESTESS POSSESSES unshakable power to reach her goals, and this power comes simply from her relentless determination to actually do what she sets out to do. While she adjusts her everyday habits and long-term trajectory as needed, she is never swayed or dissuaded from her carefully chosen path.

Sometimes we need to stop and smell the roses. But other times, we need to put our heads down and get to work.

It's possible that you're very good already at playing, resting, and being here now, so you are receiving this message because you will benefit by balancing out your relaxation with hard work. It's possible even your relaxation has not felt as satisfying as it should, or perhaps you *have* been working, but you still feel that you are spinning your wheels, and not quite getting where your heart of hearts wants to go. Whatever the case, intentional, committed effort is your answer. It will help you find your most graceful and beneficial dance of receptivity and effective forward movement.

If there's something you want to create, don't wait for inspiration to strike and your muse to suddenly appear. That's approaching the whole thing backwards. Your muse will appear when you make space for her to appear by setting aside time every day, or five days a week (or three, or whatever you can reasonably make time for), for a prescribed period.

Let's say you want to write a book. Look at your calendar and decide how much time you can reasonably spend on this project. Put this in your calendar and then stick to it. Sit at your desk for those hours and write. Show up again and again and again.

In this way, you will be holding the space for yourself to learn, improve, and ultimately succeed.

In a much shorter time than you expect, you will see your dreams and visions move out of the realm of someday and into the glorious now.

9. Oshun

BLESSINGS WILL FLOW

•

You yearn for something. This is not an expression of lack, but rather an exciting invitation to expansion. Open up to the generous flow of blessings the Goddess desires to bestow.

•

A POWERFUL ORISHA (YORUBAN DIVINITY) OF waterfalls, honey, mother's milk, affluent blessings, and all that flows, Oshun has appeared because there is something you would like to flow to you more generously: sweetness, beauty, magical wisdom, fertility, healing, wealth, or romantic love. Oshun wants you to know that when you shift from a sense of wanting into a sense of having, you will instantly open the floodgates to your good.

There is a sacred shrine to Oshun at a pilgrimage site in Oshogbo, Nigeria, where she is celebrated for protecting the town from attack. While her 12-day festival is in August, devotees also visit the shrine year-round, particularly to petition Oshun for fertility and healing, or to bless their babies and their mothers' milk as they nurse.

Ask Oshun for the form of flow that will bathe your heart in joy. If there's a waterfall or another clean, natural, moving body of water you can immerse yourself in safely, do so in tandem with your request. Also offer Oshun honey as a gesture of gratitude and faith: but always be sure to taste a little of it before you do. (Oshun loves honey, but she will only accept it if you have first put a bit on your own tongue.) You can place a jar of honey on an altar to her, or pour your honey offering into one of the streams, rivers, or waterfalls of the world.

Oshun reminds you that you miss out on all the fun stuff if you overly fixate on the final reward. Expand your view to include the whole mysterious, miraculous, and ecstatic unfolding of your heart's desire, and you will unlock the secret to magic, manifestation, and living a life of purpose. Cycles of time are not lines: they are spirals, and the whole of each spiral is contained within its every concentric swirl.

The moment you realize you wish for something, the blessing is already here. Savor the sweetness between the initial spark and its full manifestation, honoring the entire journey and letting it carry you along like a swirling, sparkling current of joy.

18. Cliodhna

THE HEART HEALS

•

Your heartbreak is temporary. With the passing of time, the pain will fade. The heart is a master at healing itself.

•

NO MATTER WHAT HAPPENS, LOVE IS ETERNAL. And even the most grievous sorrow contains an indestructible thread of radiant, shimmering beauty.

    This is the wisdom of Cliodhna (pronounced Klee-NA), the Irish goddess of life, death, love, nature, and the sea. A faerie queen, Cliodhna has been known to lure mortals into her world of eternal beauty to stay with her always. This, of course, is not a punishment but a gift.

If your heart is in pain, this is a message that your pain will eventually ebb. If you feel disconnected or numbed out, this is a message that somewhere within you, there is grief. Get in touch with this feeling and allow yourself to feel it. It may seem like your sadness will never end. But once you discover your true feelings and let them expand and move within your belly and heart, those feelings will slowly but surely lighten up like clouds in sunlight. In time, they will disperse, creating space for joy and lifting the heavy burden that has been weighing on your mind, body, and soul.

Cliodhna is always attended by her three sacred songbirds, who sing songs of healing and hope. Close your eyes for a moment. Relax your body, breathe consciously, and allow yourself to hear their etheric song. Let it improve your outlook and remind you that even after the darkest night, a new day will never fail to dawn.

Cliodhna and her songbirds also urge you to listen to heartfelt music throughout your day, and to set aside some alone time to allow your body to move to such music. Don't dance for anyone's benefit but your own. Listen to the music, breathe it into your body, and get curious about how your body would like to move. Let this sacred dance practice be a moving meditation that realigns you with your heart. This will naturally help get your emotions moving so you can finally cry, rage, or generally feel your feelings and set yourself free.

    Compassionately open up to your heartache, and you will lighten your burden of yearning. In time you will heal. The sharp pain will dissolve, and you will be left with the exquisite glow of love.

11. Eleanor of Aquitaine

BE IMPECCABLE

•

Claim your right to the throne. Impeccably embody the authority you were born to wield. Be assured that you are qualified and ready for the role destiny has chosen for you to play.

•

YOUR PRESENT TASK, PATH, OR ROLE IS BOTH challenging and significant. It will require you to draw upon all your assets and strengths. Trust your abilities, gather your troops, and be the self-possessed ruler you were born to be.

As the wife of two powerful kings, Eleanor of Aquitaine was crowned queen of two countries during her lifetime: first France, and then England. But before and beyond adopting these titles, she was an heiress and ruler in her own right as the Duchess of the vast and prosperous lands of Aquitaine, which she wisely governed throughout her long life.

Highly educated and meticulously trained in the ways of court, politics, diplomacy, and battle, Eleanor of Aquitaine was also naturally intelligent and adept. Despite kidnapping attempts and endless grabs at her status and money, Eleanor managed to outshine every other ruler of her day, significantly influencing custom, fashion, trade, tradition, and law — not just during her lifetime, but also for centuries to come.

Who are your allies? Call on them now. Also be ready to put all your wisdom, knowledge, and Goddess-given gifts to work. This is not a time to sit back and let things take their course.

Also, be honest with yourself. Is there anyone in your inner circle who may not be worthy of your trust? Look clearly at what is happening and open your eyes to false friends and deceptive maneuvers.

At the same time, strive to be impeccable in all areas. Honor your values. Balance knowledge with intuition. Be kind and fair, but also be cunning and tough. Be wise enough to recognize what you can't change, but don't hesitate for a moment to proactively change the things you can.

All the while, dress and behave with elegance. Attend to the details of your self-care and remember that your beauty is an asset and a resonant expression of your power. Take the time to burnish your presentation until you look and feel like the proud and powerful queen you are.

Eleanor of Aquitaine did not question her right and ability to rule over her world. Neither should you.

12. Etain

YOU ARE ETERNAL

●

Work with divine light to heal, transform, and be reborn. Unfetter yourself from impossible ideals of beauty and youth. Revel in your eternal radiance and timeless personal power.

●

ETAIN (PRONOUNCED Ay-DEEN) IS A CELTIC goddess and faerie queen whose name means "Shining One." Associated with both sun and moon, flowing water and luminous light, she is an alchemical goddess who reminds us that, like the caterpillar, we can always shed our present form and rise, renewed. Transformed by a romantic rival into a caterpillar, Etain then changed herself into a butterfly who was forced to live at sea for many years before being swallowed by a human queen and then being reborn, nine months later, as a mortal princess. After growing up and marrying a king, her faerie husband returned for her. The two of them transformed into swans and flew back to their magical realm.

Etain reminds you that you need never stay stuck in unpleasant feelings or situations. Even though every life will contain emergencies, challenges, and stretches of aimless boredom, you can always find a way to rise above, shake things up, and break through.

Sometimes, as we move through life's various stages, our self-worth may wobble a bit. With each new season of life, we may increase our wisdom and wealth, but we are also forced to release things we've previously treasured, such as our unwrinkled skin, our innocence, and our sparkling aura of youth.

Look now and see what Etain is showing you. With every old blessing you are asked to surrender, you can choose to see it as a way of lightening your load and breaking your chains. While it's natural to grieve the things you can never (in this lifetime) get back, you can also discover great power in letting go.

For example, while you may always naturally enjoy caring for your beauty and physical body, if you let go of the desperate need to appear a certain way in the eyes of others, imagine how much more thought-power and energy you will have to spend on simply soaking in the beauty around you and enjoying your life.

When one window of opportunity closes, there are countless more that open. Grieve your youth and past seasons if you must, but eventually set down that burden of grief. Then, open your eyes and behold the new world of liberation that awaits.

13. Li Ban

THIS IS AN INITIATION

•

Take care of yourself lovingly. You are going through a time of immense personal growth. When you emerge from your period of mourning, you will be blessed with transcendent beauty and power.

•

LI BAN (PRONOUNCED Lee-BAHN) WAS A PRINCESS of the Irish faerie race, the Tuatha De Danann. Her father had their village built around a sacred well, which flooded one night, drowning everyone except Li Ban and her dog, who were able to breathe in a tiny little cave under the flood that was now a lake. After a year of being trapped in this secluded in-between place, the great goddess Danu changed Li Ban's legs into a salmon's tail and gave her the ability to breathe underwater, effectively making her a mermaid. At the same time, her faithful little dog became an enchanted otter. Thus transformed, Li Ban and her beloved otter swam free of their subterranean refuge, continuing out of the lake and through rivers, until they reached the sea.

Receiving this card indicates that you are in your own in-between place: you have lost something or someone dear to you, and your pain has temporarily dimmed your light, your enthusiasm, and your ability to connect with others. Rest assured that this will not last forever, even if it feels like it might. Be kind and gentle with yourself, reach out for support as needed, and take care of yourself as best you can. Eventually, you too will be released from your confinement and empowered to swim free, through tributaries and waterways, until you reach the open sea.

Perhaps you have a furry family member to keep you company as you heal. But if you don't, this might be a message about adopting one if you have the time and resources to do so responsibly. You might also volunteer at an animal shelter, sign up for some therapeutic horsemanship, or offer to dog or cat sit for a friend or family member the next time they go out of town. Animals are experts at providing silent, unconditional emotional support.

This is a message of encouragement. You will heal, and you will emerge from the lonesome cave of your grief. In the meantime, take care of yourself lovingly. Every day, meditate, invoke divine support, and ask for guidance and healing.

14. Aradia

WORK YOUR MAGIC

•

Remember your power. See beyond the surface of things: into the past, future, and invisible realm. Through ritual, invocation, and intention, effect change according to your will.

•

YOU'RE A WITCH. IT'S TIME TO CLAIM AND WIELD your spiritual gifts.

This may be a nudge to plan and perform a ritual or spell, to cultivate your intuition and divination abilities, or to actively pursue your studies of magic and the occult.

Aradia is a goddess and champion of magical practitioners, appearing in an influential grimoire entitled *Aradia, or the Gospel of the Witches*. In the unique cosmology of this grimoire, Aradia's mother is Diana, mother of darkness and creator of everything, and her father is Lucifer, whose name means "light" and who is the rebellious angelic prince of spiritual illumination. Said to be born into human form in Italy in the 1300s, Aradia was burned alive by the Inquisition. But first, she learned her family's traditions and taught other women the ancient ways of magic and healing.

There are mainstream creeds that teach that it is wrong to work with Spirit to wield your authority and manifest your desires. You may also feel intimidated by the dark, the mysterious, and the vast unknown. The day might feel safe to you, while the night may appear unsettling and sinister. But it is undeniable that we are creatures of both light and darkness, the seen and unseen, life and death. Some things we can change, and others we cannot. Some truths we can know, and others will be inaccessible for as long as we live in this human form.

If you can go beyond the fear of death and the unknown, you will go beyond fear itself, and new worlds of possibility will unfold for you.

Embrace it all. Soak in the light and gaze bravely into the dark. Do not fear the power that lives in the mystery and the dance of polarity, for wielding that power is your birthright.

15. Libra Priestess

BALANCE AND BEAUTIFY

•

Release burdens of responsibility, guilt, and cumbersome belongings. Open your senses and anchor yourself in the beauty that surrounds you. Create harmony in your inner and outer worlds.

•

THE LIBRA PRIESTESS WANTS YOU TO SHED THE things that are weighing you down and holding you back. These may be inner, invisible things like needless narratives about how you have failed, what you owe someone, or who you should or shouldn't be. But they could also be tangible, physical things like gifts from an ex-partner, clothes you don't love to wear, or furniture that doesn't fit in your space.

Libra is ruled by Venus, the planet of beauty. So, this may be a message about tending to the aesthetic in your home, or bringing more consciousness to the way that you dress and present yourself to the world. The simple act of adjusting your style or décor can help you bless your life conditions and clarify your path.

Minimalism does not equate to austerity. It's merely living with the minimum of items and commitments that you, personally, desire and require. While this looks different for everyone, it will always bestow greater personal liberty. It's easier to box everything up and move to your dream house when you don't have a million things to pack. And it helps you save enough to buy your dream house when you aren't wasting your money on stuff you don't love, use, or need.

Or maybe, if you divest yourself of your assumptions, you don't really dream about a house at all. Maybe you dream about a loft, or a houseboat, or a suitcase you can carry from country to country throughout the world.

Also, take a good look at your relationships and responsibilities. Be honest. Have you incurred any of them not out of joy or true inclination, but out of a sense of duty or a misguided effort to distract yourself from who you truly are? Conversely, perhaps there are new responsibilities you would like to take on, such as a volunteer role, an exercise regimen, or a course of study.

Throw off old paradigms, let go of incumbrances, and strip yourself of all that is extra and unnecessary. Then surround yourself with true elegance and luxury, in just the way that feels right. Be deliberate about what you do and do not want, and masterfully harmonize your world.

16. Minerva

PRACTICE YOUR CRAFT

●

Regularly practice a beloved art, craft, or discipline. Be diligent as you pursue your passion. You will reap the benefits of your craftsmanship only if you have the determination to show up to your work again and again.

●

SOMETIMES IT WILL FEEL EASY, AND SOMETIMES it will feel like a slog. Regardless—whether you're a beginner, an amateur, or a master—you must train.

Minerva is the Roman goddess of arts, crafts, commerce, music, poetry, writing, math, science, logic, and the healing arts. If an avenue requires study, thought, mastery, focus, and meticulous self-cultivation, Minerva rules over it.

Divest yourself of your ego's need to impress, approach your craft with humility, and adopt a beginner's attitude and a spirit of adventure. Doing so will support your long-term success by inspiring you to show up again and again to practice and work.

Minerva punishes mortals who act out of hubris — she turned Arachne into a spider and Medusa into a gorgon. On the other hand, she rewards bold adventurers: when Ulysses and Hercules needed help during their adventures, she famously stepped in.

Minerva has also been credited with inventing numbers, medicine, and the flute.

This is a message to apply yourself more thoroughly to your chosen art, craft, hobby, or career path. Or, if you haven't chosen one yet, this could be a message to decisively make your selection and commit. Whatever you master can be a vessel for your natural brilliance. It is less important what you choose, and more important that you commit.

Some days, you will feel naturally inspired. Others, you will not. The difference between a master and a dilletante is that the master learns to push through fear, boredom, and inertia by showing up to practice, regardless of her energy level and mood.

While everyone needs to take vacations and breaks, the sunlight of mastery never shines on those who complacently wait around for inspiration to strike. Like Minerva, inspiration plays favorites: discerning between the true heroes and the folks who are just in it for the glory. The heroes don't just show up on days when their work feels like a breeze, but also on the days when it feels like a grind. They are willing to dig their ditches long before the rain begins to fall.

Call on Minerva and ask for the help you need, whether that's direction, inspiration, divine intervention, or the fortitude to regularly practice your craft.

17. Hespera
ADJUST YOUR PERSPECTIVE

•

Don't postpone pleasure until certain conditions are in place, for that day will continually elude you. Find the endless sweetness that is available to you in the present moment. Dwell in the garden of gratitude.

•

ENTER THE ORCHARD OF ETERNAL DELIGHT.
Take a bite of a crisp, golden apple.

Hespera is one of the Hesperides, the divine nymphs of the west, the sunset, and the blissful afterlife. Along with her eight sisters and her dragon brother Ladon, she guards the golden apples of love, happiness, and immortality that are so treasured by the Greek divinities.

This is a message that all the joy you could possibly desire is already here: right now. You need only open your senses to it and choose to savor it. If you believe your life needs to look a certain way before you can revel in the simple pleasure of existence, you have it backwards. The more beauty you open up to in the moment—the more you enjoy life, just as it is, with all it has to offer you now—the more you will increase your magnetism, and the more blessings you will naturally attract.

When you look back at the end of your life, it will be so easy to see that the simplest joys were the most precious: the sound of a loved one laughing, the scent of brownies baking, or the vision of sunlight sparkling on the sea.

From this vantage point, you can also see where you have been spinning your wheels. For example, by working a job you didn't like to buy stuff you didn't need, causing you to feel progressively emptier and more exhausted, even while getting 'wealthier' in the eyes of the world.

Look through Hespera's eyes and ask the wise dragon Ladon for perspective. What goals and habits can you let go of to liberate yourself from limitations and expand into the now? And how can you get better at reveling in all the precious, priceless blessings that you already possess?

Look deeply and know. Then adjust accordingly. Sensitize yourself to the magic that is life. Cultivate present-moment gratitude and you will find that you are already rich.

18. Alkonost

FLY UP AND OUT OF DRAMA

•

Lift your spirits and lighten your outlook. Elevate your gaze to the sky. Untether yourself from your present human drama and be free.

•

ALKONOST IS A RUSSIAN BIRD GODDESS WHO alights from heaven, bringing with her laughter, glad tidings, and mellifluous song. She is here to remind you that you are freer than you realize. You have the power to lift yourself up and out of painful old patterns of stagnation or struggle.

Joy is here for you: feel it. Prosperity is here for you: claim it. Let the Divine support and guide you, and allow yourself to flow through life with an ever-increasing momentum of harmonious ease.

This may be a message about releasing thoughts and beliefs that come with heavy burdens of guilt, obligation, or low self-worth. You don't have to do anything in order to be valuable. You don't have to be everything to everyone (or anything to anyone) to be precious. Let go of impossible standards, as well as any standards of worth you have placed on yourself at all.

Who you are is enough. Who you are is more than enough. Even though you are temporarily appearing in human form, in truth you are a divine being — expansive and timeless, endlessly lovable and endlessly worthy of love.

You can assist yourself in releasing such heaviness and limitation by lightening up your world, for example by clearing clutter in your home, deleting old files from your computer, and releasing unwanted responsibilities and goals.

Music can also help you change your vibration and patterning for the better. Make a point of singing, dancing, and listening to uplifting music throughout your day.

Spending time outdoors is another simple and effective way to unstick your energy and encourage your spirit to soar. When you do so, pay special attention to the air element: the flying creatures like butterflies and birds, the feeling of the breeze on your skin and in your hair, and the movement of clouds across the sky.

Alkonost has been said to bring divine guidance to the saints. Similarly, there is wisdom here about what heaven has planned for you and the divine role you have to play. Ask Alkonost for direction and insight. Then relax and trust that you'll know just what to do, whenever the time is right.

19. Redwood Queen

EXPAND INTO WEALTH

•

Expand your concept of what is possible. Expect to prosper. This will open you up to riches beyond your fondest dreams.

•

REDWOODS AND SEQUOIAS, WHICH ARE CLOSELY related, are, respectively, the tallest and biggest trees on earth. And all this size initiates with the tiniest of seeds. Even a seemingly dead redwood stump can give life to a concentric ring of baby trees.

The Redwood Queen has appeared in your reading as an omen of flourishing wealth. But she points to an important prerequisite: you must shift your view of yourself, your wealth, and your ability to thrive.

Perhaps you have previously believed that others can be wildly rich, but not you. Examine this assumption closely and you will see that it is not sound. If others have amassed prosperity, there is no reason on earth that you can't, as well.

Maybe you have perceived having great wealth as greedy, sinister, crooked, or otherwise out of alignment with integrity. In fact, while there are those who abuse the planet, its inhabitants, and its resources to get rich or stay rich, it's also true that when kind and honorable people come into wealth, it can set into motion wave after wave of momentous blessings for all.

Choose, now, to attract wealth while maintaining a standard of behavior that is wise, ethical, and just. This way, you will not have to worry about collateral damage, because you will know that when you prosper, those around you prosper. When you thrive, you set in motion greater thriving for the planet.

Clarity is available to you, along with the ability to act effectively. So, consult the Goddess in her manifestation as Redwood Queen. Ask her what actions to take to systematically and responsibly grow your empire of wealth. Then commit to your path. Be responsible and attentive around the subject of financial increase. Invest, tally, manage, and keep records. Establish conditions that will bring in money. Then work intelligently and diligently to help your money to continually grow.

Some believe that worldly wealth and spirituality do not mix, but this is an error. Money is energy: if you regard it with respect and call it in with the purest of intentions, you will experience it as a great blessing. It will allow you to support others lovingly and bring about positive change.

28. Maeve

BE FEARLESS

●

Fear nothing, and portals of power will open to you. See this challenge as an initiation. Your courage will guide you to victory.

●

THE GREAT GODDESS AND FAERIE QUEEN MAEVE is here for you, and she wants to support you in releasing all disempowering stories, paradigms, habits, relationships, and beliefs: now and in all directions of time.

Maeve wields absolute authority in all realms: faerie, human, and divine. In ancient Ireland, only she could decide who was king, and she did not hesitate to dethrone (or destroy) any king the moment he showed the least unfitness to rule. She took mortal kings as consorts, demanding total fidelity from them while simultaneously courting as many additional lovers as she chose. A goddess of love, life, death, beauty, nature, and sex, Maeve is the primordial power with dominion over all: seen and unseen, known and unknown.

Maeve reminds you that her power is not only accessible to you — it is also a part of you. It is your truest identity: your infinite aspect that was never born, never dies, and interweaves all consciousness in a glowing web of living light.

If you have been through pain or trauma recently, or if an issue from your distant past is continuing to affect you and cause your heart to ache, Maeve wants you to shift your perspective. When you face your deepest fears and most excruciating emotional pain, you always have the potential to emerge stronger, more resilient, and so much less afraid.

When you transcend even your fear of death, what can phase you? What can limit you? What can hold you back? In truth, there are no endings but only transformations from one way of being to another. But it's even truer to say: you are all incarnations of all beings at once. Right this very moment, you are one with everything that is, or ever was, or ever will be. Your human identity in this lifetime is like a little raft buffeted about in the waves, and you have temporarily forgotten that you are not just the boat, but also the wind, the sky, and the sea.

Don't fear your sexuality, your desires, or your authority. Stop worrying about what others think of you or your actions. Be unapologetic, courageous, and bold. Realize your interconnection with everything and claim your birthright as ruler of your realm.

21. Circe

YOU MAKE THE RULES

•

Make your own rules. Rebel against convention. Follow no leader other than yourself.

•

THE GREEK GODDESS CIRCE, WHOSE NAME means "enchantress," is the daughter of the ocean nymph Perse and Helios, the sun. After Zeus banished her to an island as punishment for transforming a rival nymph into a colossal sea monster, Circe transformed that lonely island into her own luxurious queendom and gloriously enchanted realm. A master of herbs and the loom, she can shapeshift into any form. When men arrive on her shores, she transforms them into the animal form that suits them most, which often turns out to be a pig.

Circe has appeared in your reading to remind you that if you don't like something, you don't have to live with it. You can instead banish it, say no to it, or transform it into something that suits you perfectly and only adds to your power. She urges you to craft your own world, to make your own rules, and to refuse to be minimized, chastened, or belittled.

If you feel limited by the expectations of your family, friends, or culture, step outside the bounds of that limitation and refuse to pay it any more mind. Everyone else can expect whatever they want from you. That doesn't mean you have to dance to their tune. Instead, move to the beat of your own groove.

Look closely at the true nature of those that are closest to you, or the folks who are related to your present circumstance or challenge. Are they truly what they appear to be? Or, deep down, might they be something else? Remember that no one is all good or all bad, and everyone contains unexplored dimensions and depth.

This may also be a message to decisively construct the home and lifestyle of your dreams, and to claim your role as absolute ruler of your own magical realm. Where do you most want to live? What type of home would you most like to spend your days in? In this ideal space, will any animals or other people live with you, or will you live alone? What styles, colors, and patterns will help you feel the most like the radiant and powerful queen you truly are?

Be like Circe. Construct your destiny, see through deception and subterfuge, and refuse to be held back by convention. You are a sorceress. Decisively and comprehensively work your magic now.

22. Angelica

PROTECT YOUR ENERGY

•

Call upon the strong, clear protection of the Goddess. Banish everything that doesn't serve you. You have the authority to choose what you do and do not want in your world.

•

THIS BLUE-EYED OWL WITH PINK GERANIUMS at her temples and chrysocolla at her brow is the embodiment of the clear, bright, and mystical energy of the angelica plant: a spiritually cleansing and protective herb which is traditionally employed in exorcisms and space clearings.

Angelica has shown up in your reading to urge you to gain clarity on what belongs in your life and what absolutely does not. Once you gain this clarity, with immense focus and determination, you must now work in both physical and energetic planes to enforce the intentions related to that clear inner knowing.

It might be abundantly obvious who or what you need to banish, exorcise, or categorically remove from your life, home, mind, or inner circle. But if you're not entirely sure, this may be a message to clean or clear clutter from your home, to purify your body and mind by eating fresh and healthy food and drinking plenty of water, or to clear the energy in your environment or aura. In turn, such healing and vibration-lifting behaviors will open your eyes to what else you need to bid farewell to and proactively prohibit from your life.

If you'd like to work with the energy of angelica in her botanical form to conjure such clearing and protective magic, diffuse a few drops of the essential oil or add them to a mister of rose water to mist your body, aura, and environment. (Just be careful if you have children, pets, or sensitive skin, as essential oils are highly potent.) Alternatively, you can place dried angelica root in a sachet and carry it, wear it, or hang it in a central location in your home. While not required, the stone chrysocolla and the herb geranium (fresh, dried, or in essential oil form) can be excellent complements to such magic.

Now and always, invoke divine support. Look deeply and discover just what you need to cleanse, banish, and protect. Then trust your intuition and do so without delay.

23. Queen Mab

GIVE YOURSELF WHAT YOU NEED

•

Set clear boundaries. Carve out time for magic and creativity. Attentively and lovingly tend to your mental and emotional health.

•

QUEEN MAB IS AN ANCIENT GODDESS AND supreme faerie queen of magic, wisdom, dreams, sleep, death, intuition, the moon, and divine feminine authority. She has appeared in your reading to encourage you to protect your time, honor your needs, and listen to the truest desires of your innermost soul.

You are naturally creative, intuitive, and empathic. While these are precious gifts to have, they are likely hard won. Natural artistic and spiritual aptitude is often found in those who have endured great pain, loss, or dysfunction. But you cannot choose to erase such suffering from your past, just as you can't give back the talents of increased sensitivity and openness that have come to you in its wake. Instead, you must learn to wield such talents wisely. This means shielding your personal energy and treating yourself with attentive and unwavering care.

If you relax, call on the Goddess, and listen deeply, you will hear and know what you need to do. It's possible that you will benefit from speaking to a therapist, getting a massage or energy healing, or taking a relaxing sea-salt bath by candlelight. Perhaps you need to spend time outdoors in nature regularly, or to take a vacation or break. There may be clear boundaries you need to set around your time or with regard to a particular relationship.

Take honest appraisal of the people, places, and situations that seem to cause you to feel drained, overwhelmed, or confused. These feelings are alerting you to opportunities to restructure your energy field, revise your relationships, and rethink the way you spend your time.

It is also imperative that you give your spiritual and creative gifts an outlet and a place to land in the physical world. Express your creativity through artistic mediums that speak to you and practice your spirituality in ways that bring you joy. Make time every day for meditation, clear and shield your energy field regularly, and express other spiritual arts—such as tarot, crystals, and spellwork—as you feel guided. You will know you are guided toward a particular practice if it gives you a boost of energy and makes you feel more alive.

You know what you need. Follow your clear inner guidance about how to take care of your mental, emotional, creative, and spiritual wellness now.

24. Scorpio Priestess

OWN YOUR SEXUALITY

●

Your sexuality is a sacred, magical current of energy. You can channel it for pleasure, influence, manifestation, and alchemical transformation. Claim it fully and let no one else siphon any portion of your power.

●

THE MAGICAL TREASURE THAT IS YOUR sexuality is not a set of behaviors to be quantified or labeled. It's not a show for others. How much or how little any given person is attracted to you or approves of you is in no way an indicator of your extrinsic value or worth.

The Scorpio Priestess reminds you that your sexual energy is synonymous with your power. That's why the outside world may attempt to steal it from you — to teach you that you should feel ashamed of it, or measure your worth based on it, or offer it to others in a specific way. There are corporations, organizations, and abusive individuals who seek to co-opt and channel your sexuality for their own selfish agenda and gain.

You are currently under the shadow of illusion. Someone or something has convinced you that your power is not safe or proper to claim or express. Perhaps you believe there is something wrong with your sexual desire or lack thereof. Maybe you think your body needs to be a certain age or weight, or to possess attractiveness in a particular form, in order to be loved, desired, or valid. Look deeply and see that such illusions come not just from fleeting values imposed upon you from the outside world, but also from fictional conditions that have nothing to do with you anyway: what you imagine others to feel, think, or believe.

Set an inner boundary now. Refuse to be held back or minimized by these specters of social anxiety and cultural prejudice. Not only are they restrictive and small-minded: they are also false. Send them back, now, to the native nothingness from whence they came by refusing to entertain them for one moment more.

If you feel pressure to behave a certain way, sexually or otherwise, this will cause you to feel drained. Step back from any behaviors you feel compelled to display and reconnect with your innermost self. Instead of asking yourself what others want, or how you can validate your worth in their eyes, ask yourself: what do I want? What feels good to me? Without outside pressure or standards, how do I want to experience the joy of being in my body and the pleasure of being alive? The answers to such questions will illuminate your path.

25. Morgan le Fay

EMBODY THE DIVINE FEMININE

•

Study the magical and healing arts. Cast spells and perform rituals to shift and shape reality according to your will. Be the priestess you were born to be and honor the Great Goddess in all that you do.

•

MORGAN LE FAY IS THE PRIESTESS OF THE SACRED island of Avalon and the goddess of the Celtic afterlife and Otherworld. Featured prominently in the Arthurian legends, Morgan le Fay likely predates the King Arthur stories, presiding since ancient times as the primordial goddess of magic, healing, life, death, visions, dreams, the moon, water, and the earth.

Morgan le Fay wants you to understand that you have an important role to play in your own life and in the spiritual evolution of the planet. This role can best be described as priestess. Until you claim this role and live it, you will not quite feel like yourself. So, make time every day (or most days) for your spiritual and magical work. This means sitting down for at least 10 minutes to pray, meditate, visualize, chant, or otherwise devote your time and attention to the realm of the sacred.

Balance is of the essence. On the one hand, taking yourself and your spirituality too seriously will be detrimental to your purpose. But on the other hand, it's important to notice and adjust if you're not taking your path seriously enough. Be light about your practice. Don't cling to dogma and don't hesitate to laugh at yourself along the way. But also give your spirituality the time and attention it needs in order to thrive.

Temporary flights and forays into spirituality can be exciting and fun, but showing up daily will significantly shift your energy, broaden your perspective, and improve the quality of your life.

So: choose a course of magical study and pursue it. Learn about Goddess spirituality. Practice it and place your attention on it, over and over again. Construct an altar to the Goddess. Offer gifts to her like incense, flowers, and candles, as well as vibrational gifts like prayers, songs, and sacred chants.

Give to the Goddess and she will always give back. Love the Goddess and you will feel the love. Awaken to the Goddess and she will awaken her infinite wisdom within you.

26. Samovila

HEAL THE PLANET

•

Attune to the pristine spirit of nature and take guided action to heal the planet. Sensitize yourself to the subtle web of light that is the interconnected consciousness of everything. Doing so will show you how you can help bring about positive, effective, and lasting change.

•

SAMOVILA IS THE NATURE GODDESS WHO presides over the Russian, Macedonian, and Bulgarian female fae spirits known as the Vilas or Samovili. Although these enchanting nature goddesses were once universally revered, with the advent of Christianity and the patriarchy, they began to inspire fear. They were often blamed for illness, crop failure, and other misfortune, and it was said they would employ their beguiling beauty to trick men and lure them to their death.

But Samovila and her mesmerizing entourage are not malevolent. They are simply protective of the natural world in all its diverse and delicate complexity. Much like the unicorn, who can only be seen in untouched nature and who exclusively bestows her magical boons upon the valiant and true, Samovila's intentions are pure. Also like the unicorn, she can be fierce and unforgiving when appropriate, and she will not hesitate to defend her realm.

This card is a clear message to act with integrity. Choose a career or volunteer position that allows you to work diligently on behalf of plants, animals, the planet, and wellness of the natural world. Align your daily behaviors and habits with the environmentalist cause. For example, eat fewer animal products, choose organic fruits and vegetables when possible, and generally reduce your waste and carbon emissions as much as you possibly can.

This may also be a mission to purify your personal energy and to realign your motivations with the highest level of honor. Relax, breathe rhythmically, settle your mind, and ask Samovila to remove any stuck, heavy, or frenetic energy from your aura. Ask her how you can recalibrate your values and approach your current situation with the most impeccable possible standards and intentions. Continue to relax and breathe slowly as you allow yourself to see, hear, sense, or know precisely how to proceed.

Consistently behave with integrity and you will embody the truest expression of success.

27. Oak Queen

TAKE A BREAK

•

Take a break. Get grounded. Balance your hard work with relaxation, connection, and play.

•

YOU HAVE BEEN WORKING HARD: DOING YOUR best to keep up with your to-do lists and focus on your goals. The Oak Queen admires your work ethic — in fact, she shares it herself. But she also knows that true success is always achieved in tandem with joy. And you cannot sustain your joy if you lose sight of the everyday moments that make life so precious and lush.

Oaks are regal, strong, and allied with the sun. In magical herbalism and Celtic mythology, they are aligned with prosperity and success. According to vibrational medicine, the subtle energy of oak flowers helps you recharge and balance out after a period of exhaustion or extended work.

The Oak Queen counsels you to let the earth nourish you. Let the sunshine warm you and the cool breeze enliven you. Let yourself dream in the light of the moon. Balance your duty with enjoyment, and your single-minded focus with expansive laughter and love.

There is great value in being responsible. It's honorable to follow through on your promises. But you're a living creature, not a machine. When you feel overwhelmed or out of touch, it's okay to bow out of commitments and plans. Constant effort is not sustainable. Why are you working so hard, after all, if you never take the time to connect deeply with your loved ones or to soak in the magic of life?

Even if you view your work as an expression of your love for those you provide for, when you miss out on leisurely moments with those same loved ones, you miss out on so much. And so do they! The people who love you want to simply be with you more than they want the resources and financial blessings you can provide.

If you check your phone constantly for messages and social media developments, this would be an obvious habit to curb in order to create more space in your schedule for holistic replenishment. Duties and chores take up enough of your attention: why fritter the rest of it away with unnecessary screen time? Power down your phone and soak up the abundant beauty and love that surround you even now.

Admit it: you need a break. Take some downtime to relax your body and mind. Recalibrate the balance between work and the rest of your life so you can restore your enthusiasm for both.

28. Sinann

DON'T WAIT FOR PERMISSION

•

Be true to your desires. Do what you know you must do. Listen to, and act on, the innermost stirrings of your heart.

•

DON'T WAIT FOR THE POWERS THAT BE TO GIVE you permission to follow your heart. There are times when you must break the rules to bring forth vital new channels of prosperity and possibility.

Sinann is the living spirit of the River Shannon, the longest and grandest river in Ireland, which spans 17 counties and enlivens all of Ireland with a singular and sacred magic.

Sinann was once a brilliant young princess: wise and learned in all subjects and disciplines. But she wanted more — she wanted to know the transcendent truth of everything. So, she attempted to drink from the Well of Connla, which would bless her with the infinite wisdom she desired.

As the story is often told, females were forbidden to touch the Well of Connla. In response to her defiant attempt, the well overflowed, creating the majestic River Shannon. Sinann the princess was drowned, but Sinann the goddess was born. To this day, she is a river that flows through Ireland ceaselessly, bestowing all her many gifts upon the land.

Like Sinann, your path may not initially be smooth. You may feel that you are forbidden to go where you want to go or believe you are barred from seeking what you dearly desire to obtain.

Notice that the Well of Connla did not rear back with Sinann's supposedly forbidden approach. If she wasn't allowed to touch it, why would it reach up and touch her? And not only touch her, but also engulf her, merge with her spirit, and bless Ireland with its most sacred waterway? Perhaps because Sinann was not, in the truest sense, forbidden to touch the well at all. That was the false story she needed to rebel against in order to fulfill her divinely appointed role.

Similarly, when you recognize the boundary but move forward anyway, you may be required to undergo a challenge, initiation, and transformation. Your success, and your path to that success, will likely look different to what you could have foreseen.

Invoke divine support, act with daring decisiveness, and move forward into your destiny. Forge the path that is illuminated by your soul.

29. Arianrhod

HEAL WITH THE MOON

•

Take care of yourself. Deep healing is available to you. Access this healing and enter a time of profound renewal and hope.

•

ARIANRHOD, WHOSE NAME MEANS "SILVER Wheel" (a moniker for the moon), is a Welsh incarnation of the Great Goddess. She embodies the lunar energies of healing, magic, mystery, intuition, and receptivity. She is the primordial power that gave birth to the spirits of the sun and the sea.

Much like *The Star* in the Tarot, receiving this card means you are on an upswing and are on course for wellness and success. While much of your healing journey may still be in front of you, if you invoke divine support and allow yourself to receive it, a desirable outcome will certainly unfold.

This is also a clear sign to seek and allow support from healers and friends in the physical world.

Light a white, off-white, or silver candle to Arianrhod, or simply relax, breathe, and ask her for her help. Speak words from your heart about precisely the type of healing you need or the holistic success you desire. Then relax even more and set the intention to allow Arianrhod's powerful guidance and nourishing light to flow in. Breathe this energy into your body and energy field and feel your whole being transforming into silvery lunar light.

Afterwards and in the days ahead, follow your intuition about how and where to seek further support. Perhaps you will feel guided to schedule an energy healing, a therapy session, or an appointment with your doctor. Or maybe you sense that you need to spend more time in nature, drink more water, or consume more fresh vegetables and healing herbal teas.

It's a good idea to attune your healing efforts to the phases of the moon. Set healing intentions at the new moon, sense your immunity and strength expanding during the waxing moon, bless yourself in the light of the full moon, and release old unwanted conditions and issues as the moon wanes.

Be proactive about your inner and outer health. Work with Arianrhod and the moon, take loving care of yourself, and patiently allow your healing journey to unfold.

38. Stella Maris

YOU ARE SAFE

•

No matter how things may currently appear, you are protected. Call upon divine support and trust your inner guidance system. The Goddess will deliver you to safety.

•

EVEN IF IT FEELS AS IF YOUR LITTLE BOAT IS being tossed about in a stormy sea, don't be afraid. For Stella Maris' appearance in your reading means you will not, ultimately, lose your way. The waves will not engulf you. You will not be dashed upon the rocks.

Stella Maris means "Star of the Sea." Appearing to sailors and seafarers of various cultures to help rescue them, protect them, and correct their course, she has been called the names of several goddesses (such as Mary, Yemaya, and Kuan Yin), perhaps revealing that the mother goddesses with whom she is identified are ultimately one and the same.

If you will but allow her, Stella Maris will shield you from harm, steer you toward calmer waters, and help you discover the best route to your most ideal destination.

In this image, Stella Maris is depicted with a crown of clear quartz crystals: a protective stone that helps focus your mind and energize your intentions. Her companion is a water dragon, a profoundly magical spirit animal who can further bless you with healing, renewal, wisdom, abundant wealth, and a shielding circle of light.

Close your eyes, breathe, clear your mind, and let your body unclench. Trust that Stella Maris will lift you up and out of danger and bestow upon you all the boons you require. You don't need to know all the details of how this will unfold. Simply relax, let go, and allow yourself to receive this help.

If it feels difficult to trust that things are working out as they should, help your relaxation along by taking a sea-salt or Epsom-salt bath, playing uplifting music, or spending time in nature. You can also support yourself in receiving Stella Maris' blessings by lighting her a blue candle or by offering her the scent of roses or vanilla in the form of incense or essential oil.

Everyone, at times, encounters rough waters in the sea of life. But Stella Maris is here for you, so be encouraged. She will help you emerge safely from the storm.

31. Eagle Priestess

CHANNEL THE HIGHEST LIGHT

•

Connect with the pure light of the infinite sun. See the whole picture from the highest possible perspective. Still your mind, work your magic, and attune to the guidance that will bring about the best outcome for all concerned.

•

THE EAGLE PRIESTESS' GAZE IS VAST.
Shapeshifting into the queen of birds, she reigns over the sky. Simultaneously, she communes with spirit high

above as she looks with wisdom at the broad expanse of the earth so far below.

The Eagle Priestess asks you to work similar magic now. Rise above the petty part of you that seeks to make yourself special or right at the expense of what is ultimately best. Recognize and release the desire to manipulate others through people-pleasing, falsely impressing, or otherwise concealing your true motivations and preferences.

Relax, breathe, and envision an infinite sun at the center of everything. Send your consciousness into the heart of this sun. Then listen deeply as your awareness is permeated by the highest and most glorious truth. Perceive this truth comprehensively — with all your inner senses, including clairaudience (clear hearing), clairsentience (clear feeling), and clairvoyance (clear seeing).

In deliberately connecting to Divinity in this way, your personal energy field will shift. Your chakras will align, your aura will be strengthened, and you will come into resonance with the divine aspect of you: the part of you that is one with everything, which is Who You Really Are.

From this place, you will know just what to do. It will take less effort than you expected, but will be exponentially more effective and will yield the most positive possible results.

A visitation from the Eagle Priestess is an auspicious omen, for it means all the power of the heavens is available to you. Claim that power now. Let go of ego attachment. Then, clear your mind, steady your spirit, and channel the highest light.

32. Caer Ibormeith

BE INDEPENDENT

•

Be independent. Be brave and speak your truth. You cannot connect authentically with others if you do not show who you are and state what you need.

•

DIVINE ROMANCE AND TRUE FRIENDSHIP ARE not for the fearful or faint of heart.

Caer Ibormeith, whose name means "Yew Berry," is a shapeshifting goddess: she appears sometimes in human form and sometimes as a swan. While in swan form, she spied the Celtic god of love, known as Angus Mac Og. She then appeared to him in dreams as a beautiful woman by a lake, and proceeded to bewitch him. When he finally found her in waking life, he proposed. She promised to marry him with one condition: that he, too, would learn to transform into a swan. On Samhain, he did. To this day, they live together in marital bliss, soaring between the worlds of life and death, form and spirit, waking life and the land of dreams.

Similarly, the love or companionship you desire is not one in which you lose yourself. Agreeing for agreement's sake is a sure path to loneliness. Without speaking up about who you are, what's true for you, and what you need, you do not offer the chance for your friend, family member, or partner to get to know you. And without being known, how can you be loved?

Desire, too, fades when you try to become so aligned with your partner, you lose your sense of what makes you distinct.

Caer Ibormeith knew that to live happily, she must retain her swan identity and her ability to fly beyond the veil and between the worlds. She sensed, also, that her beloved would benefit from the wisdom and depth such a skill would bestow. While she hoped he would agree to her demand, she didn't know for sure what he would do. Though she was besotted with him, if he had refused to join her as part swan, or if he had insisted that she instead stay in her human form, she was ready to turn him down and bid him a permanent adieu.

    Seek to connect but remember that true connection can only happen between two individuals. If you dissolve your identity into that of another, you will lose your ability to relate and in time, the relationship will end or your enthusiasm for the partnership will fade.

33. Queen Victoria

TRIUMPH OVER BULLIES

•

Don't let the bullies win. Lay down the law.
Refuse to cower in fear.

•

QUEEN VICTORIA'S MOTHER KNOWINGLY AND systematically isolated and emotionally abused Victoria throughout her childhood, seeking to keep her and her future authority in thrall. But in the end, it didn't work. Upon becoming queen at age 18, Victoria banished her mother from her life and presence as much as she legally could, reasserting her right and ability to make her own choices, marry who she wanted, and govern according to her will.

Portrayed here in her youthful aspect with her beloved cat, White Heather, Victoria reminds you that you were born with the divine right to rule over your own life and affairs. The queen, like her cat, retained her autonomy, with no intention whatsoever to capitulate to the designs or opinions of those who attempted to control her.

Do not allow the outside world—your family, friends, partner, strangers, your community, or societal convention—to pressure you to act in any way. Similarly, do not wait for them to validate you. Validate yourself. Know what feels right to you and stick to your choices and convictions.

Also, remember that no matter who someone is to you, you have no obligation to make yourself available for their mistreatment. Some dysfunctional relationships can be healed or repaired. Others cannot. Don't keep trying to change someone who doesn't want to change. Don't keep trying to fix something that can't be fixed. If someone continually abuses you or refuses to honor your boundaries, don't stick around for it. Be like a regal cat: unapologetically pick yourself up and walk away.

Finally, trust in your ability to learn and adapt. Just because it might feel intimidating to go out on your own or to learn a new, essential life skill, it doesn't mean you can't do it. You can. So, prepare to go your own way and let go of limiting beliefs about what you can and can't do. You will certainly surprise yourself with your aplomb, your hidden talents, and your considerable aptitude for success.

34. Black Annis

YOU'RE NOT FOR EVERYONE

•

*Find your fierceness. Recover your wildness.
Release the need to be universally liked.*

•

BLACK ANNIS IS A SHAPESHIFTING WITCH goddess native to Leicestershire County, England. She sometimes appears as a woman, sometimes as a giant black cat, and sometimes a cross between the two. She is said to appear with a terrifying visage, waiting to abduct and eat naughty children who are wandering alone after dark. But this was just a cautionary tale used by parents to keep children from misbehaving or leaving their homes. In truth, Black Annis is a primordial goddess of nature and magic, whose rites may have been forgotten but who lives on, dwelling in the cave that was possibly once her shrine.

You may have received this card because you feel your motives to be unfairly mistrusted or your true nature to be misunderstood. Black Annis understands this conundrum well. She wants you to know you are not alone: unique, gifted, creative, and intuitive folks are (and have been) feared and marginalized far too often, for far too long. She counsels you to clarify, to yourself, who you really are. Don't let others' presumptions and prejudice color your self-image. Though not everyone will understand you, if you are true to yourself, there will certainly be those who see you, get you, and respect you for who you are.

Furthermore, don't allow your light to be dimmed or your voice to be silenced by the fears or expectations of others. If you're angry, let your anger burn. If you're impatient with injustice, make your feelings known. If you see things in a way that others don't, be brave enough to patiently but assertively share your perspectives and take action on behalf of positive change.

As a largely solitary nature goddess, Black Annis knows that spending time alone can help you hear your guidance, recalibrate your outer actions with your core inner values, and remember who you are. So, it's a good idea to schedule some quiet alone time without technology or other distractions, ideally in nature. Relax, feel the earth recharging you, and connect with your courage, wisdom, and innermost self.

35. Aries Priestess

BUST THROUGH BLOCKS

•

Assert your personal power. Refuse to be held back. See life as one big adventure, containing countless opportunities for exploration and growth.

•

THE ARIES PRIESTESS HAS SHOWN UP IN YOUR reading to remind you to bust through blocks with a spirit of playful exuberance. Shake up the areas where you feel bored or stuck.

While being a responsible adult is not a bad thing, sometimes your idea of what that means can hold you back from expressing who you really are.

If it appears you have no options that will allow you to achieve a desire or goal, never ever believe it. Be like the fox: be wily and make your own luck. Go beyond the conventional and expected responses to any challenge and make a way where there (seemingly) is no way.

The butterflies that surround the Aries Priestess indicate that a positive transformation is at hand, but you must let go of old patterning and worn-out expectations if you want to experience all the fresh blessings that await. Surrender the need to see every step of the journey so you can make space for something astonishing and unexpected.

Aries has an audacious and independent nature, so this is not a time to go along with the herd. Perhaps it's time to stop being a follower and instead become a leader. Or, you may simply be guided to claim your own direction and set off on your own path.

The Aries Priestess loves surprises and hates spoilers. She wants you to be blessed with a spectacular outcome you could never have previously foreseen. Claim this future by taking decisive action. Don't worry so much about what to do: just start. You can always adjust your strategy as needed.

It's a thrilling feeling to make your own way in the world while allowing yourself to learn as you go, and it frees up so much positive potential when you do so. So don't hold back! Be proactive, courageous, and bold.

36. Aspen Princess
DANCE WITH CHANGE

•

Create harmony through embracing polarities. Honor the old but look toward the new. Dance gracefully with change.

•

SOMETIMES YOU WILL BE SHY, INTROVERTED, and withdrawn. Other times you will share your beauty generously and playfully with the world. And that beauty will change throughout your life: youthful spring green becomes the glowing gold of maturity. All the while, you can revel in the constant change of seasons, knowing you are still the same lovable being at your core.

All the seasons have their value. Each stage of life makes the others distinct, setting off their unique charms. Spring is filled with romance and possibility. Summer inspires adventure and liveliness. Fall asks us to reflect, connect, and prepare to go within. Winter tempts us to rest, recharge and sip on hot chocolate by the crackling fire.

In spring, aspens are an eye-catching peridot green. In summer, they deepen to emerald. In fall, they burnish to gold. Meanwhile, their leaves dance endlessly in even the smallest breeze, often shimmering with the diamond-white light of the sun. Throughout the winter, aspens are still, leafless, and bone-white. Alive but resting. Retreating from the surface of life to replenish themselves at their innermost core.

The Aspen Princess asks you to assess: what do you need now in order to dance with the seasons of life, nurture yourself, and thrive? Sometimes, when you have the impulse to stay in for the night, it's the right choice for you because you need some quality alone time to refresh and renew. Other times, though, it's simply inertia: you would nourish yourself best by overcoming your reticence, putting on your party dress, and making the extra effort to join in the fun.

We all need community and connection, just like we all need quiet alone time to recharge. But receiving this card means it might be time to honor where you've been while proactively taking a step toward something new. If you've been staying in, it might be time to go out. If you've been going out, it might be time to stay in. Changing your momentum always feels, at first, cumbersome. That's why we can feel a little sniffly or groggy when winter turns to spring, or when summer turns to fall. But then the season gains its own happy pace and carries you along in its scintillating flow.

37. Melusine

YOU NEED QUIET TIME

•

Quietly go within. Delight in your true self and your direct experience of life, without feeling the need to narrate, document, or explain. Nourish your spirit with your own silent and secret joy.

•

MELUSINE IS A FRENCH WATER GODDESS. RAISED on the sacred Isle of Avalon, she one day ventured into the forest in Poitou, France, and decided to bathe in a well. A nobleman came upon her, fell in love instantly, and proposed. She agreed to marry him as long as he promised to leave her alone every Saturday. After bearing him ten sons, one Saturday rolled around and her husband's curiosity got the best of him. What he saw when he spied on her astounded him: while bathing, she shapeshifted into a water dragon. When she discovered that he had failed to honor her one condition, she flew (on her dragon's wings) back to Avalon, secretly returning at night to nurse her two youngest sons.

Melusine was a loving and devoted wife and mother. At the same time, she knew her well-being depended on regular alone time during which she could let herself fully inhabit her water dragon form. She wasn't ashamed of who she was — she just knew that expanding into her true self required no audience. By taking the time she needed to get to know the silent truth of her being, she could draw upon that truth as required throughout the remainder of the week.

Similarly, your authenticity is highly personal. While staying true to yourself does sometimes require assertiveness and self-disclosure, it never requires over-sharing. In fact, attuning to yourself and your needs often results in the desire to pull back, stay silent, or set boundaries around your time.

If you're inquiring about a relationship, this is a message to retain your independence and honor your need for quiet alone time. If you're asking about a project, goal, or creative endeavor, don't feel pressure to immediately broadcast your ideas or offer some form of tangible content to the world. First, retreat. Relax into silence. Get in touch with your true motivation and your joy. Then, when the time is right, you will know who you are, so you will know just how to proceed.

38. Verdandi

NOW IS THE TIME

●

Stop obsessing about the past or worrying about the future. Anchor yourself in the present. Inhabit your body and be exactly where you are.

●

WHILE YOU REMEMBER THE PAST AND anticipate the future, these only exist as concepts in your mind. Truly, there is only ever one moment: now.

Verdandi, whose name means "becoming," is one of the three Norns in Norse mythology. More powerful even than the gods, the Norns are three sisters who tend to Yggdrasil, the World Tree, and tirelessly weave our fate. Urd is the Norn of the past, Skuld is the Norn of the future, and Verdandi is the Norn of the ever-present now.

While you can certainly heal and learn from your past and effect positive change in your future, the only time you can do either of these things is now. So don't get so distracted by thoughts about the past or future that you neglect to access the magic that exists only in the present. And take care not to postpone your happiness by placing conditions on your joy.

Take a deep breath and notice the scent of the air and the way it feels in your nostrils, chest, and belly. Tune in to your body and feel gravity anchoring you into the earth. Gaze at the trees dancing in the breeze and the clouds moving through the sky. Accept everything that's here now, within you and outside of you. Claim it. Weave it into the pattern. Let it be.

If you look back on your life experience, you can see how happenings that appeared random or even unfortunate turned out to have silver linings you never could have foreseen. You can also reflect on times that you worried incessantly about things that never actually happened, or that did happen, but turned out to be fine. So don't waste time on regrets, and don't fritter away your life force worrying about things you can't control.

Once you connect with a sense of mindful presence, if you feel guided to act, act. If you feel guided to wait, wait. If you feel guided to be still, be still.

You can help establish mindful presence through meditation, spending time in nature, unplugging from technology, or simply taking a few deep, conscious breaths. Deliberately let go of worries, disempowering stories, and anything else that siphons off your energy and distracts you from your moments of joy.

39. Freya

HOLD ON TO YOUR CENTER

•

Don't lose yourself or "fall head over heels." Hold on to your center. Pay attention—in each moment—to what is actually happening and to your ever-changing feelings, opinions, and desires.

•

WHEN PASSION DEVOLVES INTO NEEDINESS and desperation, you will miss important information because you are so distracted by your fluttering heart.

And, if you hide or amend your true self, no one can know you — so how can you truly be loved?

Freya, whose name translates to "Lady," is the Divine Feminine aspect in the Norse pantheon. She is both love goddess and war goddess: goddess of beauty and death. A shapeshifting spirit who delights in the magical arts, she is credited with teaching Odin how to work magic. For centuries, she has been honored and beloved by witches.

Despite the fear, censure, and condemnation that was widely directed toward her at the advent of Christianity, Freya didn't go anywhere. She retained her name recognition and unique essence, refusing to be syncretized, assimilated, or banished. This day, when we choose to venerate Freya, we know who we are venerating: a goddess of immense power who stands for fearlessness, independence, and passionate love.

When you care about a relationship, taking a stand for who you are is always a vulnerable feeling. That's because we want so much to be accepted, especially by those we respect and admire. But the irony is that when we hide who we are out of fear, we end up feeling invisible, which is a very different thing than feeling loved. This is why love requires valor. Without the bold act of being yourself, you will always be lonely, no matter who stands by your side. In fact, you will even end up alienating yourself.

While it's true that you can't control the choices or actions of others, you can control how you show up in your interactions, and how much respect you show to yourself as you do. In time, when you make a habit of knowing your truth and living from your authenticity, the relationships that are not aligned with you will fall away, and the relationships that are best for you will naturally gravitate into your sphere. Trusting this process is the basis of true self-respect.

Be brave. Be yourself. Live from these straightforward, self-honoring values, and you will unlock the love you desire.

48. Elizabeth Woodville

REIGN WITHOUT APOLOGY

•

Who you are is not up for debate. No one can divine your motivations or innermost thoughts. Do not allow the world to define your value, your rank, or your authority to rule.

•

EVEN THOUGH ELIZABETH WOODVILLE'S mother was a countess and her father was a duke, she was still considered by the English aristocracy to be middle class.

Early in his reign, the young and newly crowned King Edward IV married Elizabeth Woodville secretly. He kept it under wraps because he knew the marriage was against the designs and wishes of his family and advisors, who had fought so ruthlessly to put him on the throne.

This made Elizabeth the first "commoner" to become Queen of England.

Elizabeth Woodville has appeared here to remind you that no matter where you come from, what you look like, or how much money or prestige your family of origin had or didn't have, you have the right and ability to wield your authority with confidence.

Others can assume whatever they want about you: that doesn't make their assumptions true. Notice where the beliefs or expectations of others may be inappropriately imposing themselves upon your self-image. You are the only one who gets to define who you are.

Similarly, if someone else is trying to tell you your own thoughts, feelings, or motivations, be on the alert. This is a sure sign of malignant manipulation and control. You know why you are doing and saying the things that you are doing and saying, and you can go ahead and trust that your inner experience is indeed your own. No one else is inhabiting your body, mind, and spirit. No one else can tell you what you think, what you feel, or what it's like to be you.

Be proud of who you are, exactly as you are. Compare yourself to no one. Rule over your life with autonomy and pride. Let no one hinder your belief in your Goddess-given right to reign.

41. Angrboda

FIND YOUR SANCTUARY

•

There is a hidden magic within your current situation. Find inner stillness and inhabit your inner sanctuary. Channel disappointment into the motivation to try again.

•

WHILE ANGRBODA'S NAME MEANS "BRINGER OF sorrow," she is also the Norse goddess who bestows an apple of fertility upon couples who ask for divine help with conceiving a child. A shapeshifting spirit who has given birth to both wolves and powerful gods, she was burned on a spit by a group of rival gods three times. Although expected to perish in the fires, each time she reappeared unharmed. To avoid the continued wrath of her rivals, she now lives safely in her own protected realm: a mystical forest known as The Iron Wood.

No matter what challenges you've endured in the past, Angrboda wants you to find your own inspiration to rise from the fire, renewed. While you can certainly feel your feelings related to any injustices you've been subjected to, don't let the unfairness of the past hold you back from living up to your full potential in the present. You can see your past hurts as burdens and barricades, or you can see them as opportunities to dissolve, reform, and emerge wiser, more radiant, and more determined than ever before.

This may be a message to move elsewhere and distance yourself from hostile environments and dysfunctional dynamics. When wolves, ravens, and other wild animals encounter mistreatment, they don't stick around to try to convince their tormentors to stop. Provided their lives are not in immediate danger, wild animals don't even stay to fight. They simply leave and find a safe territory where they can be themselves and live in peace.

Even if you're not sure if you want to leave a relationship, role, or physical location, you will benefit from spending some quiet time alone so you can reconnect with yourself and discover your deepest inner truth. Turn off your phone, go somewhere quiet and safe, perhaps light a candle or gaze at the trees, and listen to the ever-present wisdom of your soul.

Draw upon your will to triumph and your unbending drive to succeed. Take the time you need to offer yourself compassion and connect with your truth. If you fulfill these promises to yourself, Angrboda assures you: victory will be yours.

42. Mary, Queen of Scots
GUARD YOUR THRONE

●

Guard your throne. One or more people in your sphere fear your power. Be alert to any attempts to undermine your self-confidence or usurp your Goddess-given right to rule.

●

MARY, QUEEN OF SCOTS WANTS TO HELP YOU along on your path to your own personal throne, where you are the uncontested ruler over your world. Tragically doomed to suffer grave injustices in her own life, in her spirit form, this queen can help us to first detect, and then triumph over, prejudice, jealousy, unfairness, inequality, guile, and deceit.

Since birth, Queen Mary Stuart was pummeled with vicious attempts to steal, squelch, borrow, or siphon off her power.

Look deeply at your current situation. Are your allies truly your allies? Which ones are helping you, and which ones may be secretly plotting to destabilize or usurp your power?

Mary was subjected to the treachery and treason of some of her closest allies and family members, including her half-brother, her most trusted advisor, and the father of her child. Removed from the throne and hidden away on house arrest for many years, she was eventually beheaded under the authority of Queen Elizabeth.

Luckily, Mary, Queen of Scots has appeared to help you triumph and become even more powerful than you otherwise could have been.

But first, be aware that in one way or another, things may not be quite what they seem. A friend may be a foe. Compliments may be subtle digs or attempts to manipulate you. Someone who has volunteered to "take you under their wing" or "show you the ropes" may be attempting to undercut your confidence, distract you from surpassing them, or otherwise influence your behavior for their own selfish gain.

No one has perfect boundaries all the time. We are all learning as we go and doing the best with what we know. But clarity is here for you and the power in this situation belongs to you. So don't waste energy worrying, complaining, or beating yourself up — just notice what's happening, ask Mary, Queen of Scots for help, and follow your intuition about how to proceed. Then take swift and decisive action on your own behalf.

43. Ostara

SEEDS WILL SPROUT, FLOWERS WILL BLOOM

•

Fabulous potential abounds. Seeds of prosperity are sprouting. Your world is about to burst forth into riotous bloom.

•

OSTARA, GODDESS OF SPRING, SHARES HER NAME with the sabbat that falls on the spring equinox: the day when the days and nights are of roughly equal length, and the portal through which the light begins to dominate the dark. At spring, she generously casts her lush green cloak across the earth, sowing seeds and bringing forth life.

This is a lucky omen, indicating that whatever you are experiencing or inquiring about will prosper and thrive. Even if you can't see the fruits of your labor quite yet, continue to plant seeds and tend to the sprouts. In time, your garden will surely flourish.

If you're asking about a romantic relationship, love is in the air. If it's a budding relationship, look forward with joyful anticipation and have fun with the springtime of your love. If it's an established one, cultivate laughter, plan an adventure together, and generally draw upon creativity, spontaneity, and passion to rekindle the fresh exhilaration that was there at the start.

Ostara is a goddess of fertility and expansion, so this may be a message to invest in your future in some significant way. Start something new, such as a business, a career path, or a savings account. If you've been considering buying a house, applying for college, or investing in the stock market, now might be the time to put that goal into action.

What ideas or possibilities cause your heart to swell? Perhaps there's something you would love to do or try but have previously dismissed as a pipe dream: too wonderful to be possible, too good to be true, or otherwise just out of reach. In truth, if your heart of hearts shows you a vision of resplendent joy and success, that's a possible future for you, provided you ask the Divine to support you in making your dream a reality. As you do so, relax and smile. Then, when you feel guided to, boldly act.

The precise action you take is less important than the initiative itself. The idea is to put things in motion, keep them in motion, and gain momentum over time.

First, plant the seeds. Then, day after day, offer them water, sunshine, and plenty of love. In perfect timing and sooner than you expect, they will surely grow.

44. Isis

MANIFEST A MIRACLE

•

Manifest the miracle that is on the horizon for you. Claim the blessing that will bring you delight. Ask the Goddess for help and tap into the limitless potential your future holds.

•

A WISH WILL BE GRANTED. THIS GLORIOUS outcome will be beyond what you have previously envisioned or expected.

Isis is perhaps the most beloved and revered incarnation of the Great Goddess in known history. Egyptian in origin, her worship spans cultures, continents, and millennia. She is the Queen of Heaven and Earth, a goddess who loves all, nourishes all, and brings great boons and benefits to her devotees. She is known to be particularly compassionate because she is not just the queen of everything, she is also every woman, every person, and every being, from the tiniest spider to the grandest tree. Beyond time and space, she has lived every life — is living every life experience there is now, has been, and will be.

Light Isis a candle. Relax, breathe, and center your mind. Inwardly see or sense Isis' compassionate gaze. Thank the goddess for all that you already have. Then, still in the present tense, thank her once more: this time, for the object of your hope, need, or desire. Say, "Isis, thank you for [the condition you are requesting]." Feel an upwelling of even more gratitude for this miraculous blessing, as if it is already here. Indeed, feel and trust that it is certainly on its way to you now.

Isis is a teacher of magic: the high priestess of all magical, spiritual folk. So, she can also help you to own and wield your spiritual power. Ask her for guidance on how to best express your spiritual path and expect to be guided in perfect timing and unmistakable ways. You might see signs or symbols in the physical world, you might be drawn to certain teachings, or someone might invite you to a spiritual gathering or talk.

Your magic is your own. Your life experience is an expression of that magic. Allow yourself to know and claim your needs, wants, hopes, dreams, and desires. Ask Isis for help, and then feel the joyful expectation that the help you've requested is already on its way.

About the Author

Photo © Whitney DeVoto / @devotophoto

TESS WHITEHURST believes life is magical. In addition to authoring this deck, she's the author of *The Halloween Forever Oracle*, *The Oracle of Daydreams and Moonbeams*, *The Oracle of Portals*, *Cosmic Dancer Oracle*, *The Queen Mab Oracle*, *The Magic of Flowers Oracle*, and *The Angel Magic Oracle*.

Tess's books include the bestselling *Magical Housekeeping*, the brand new *Radiant: Embracing Your Power and Beauty at Midlife*, and lots of other fan favorites such as *You Are Magical*, *The Good Energy Book*, and *The Magic of Flowers*. Articles she has written have appeared in *Writer's Digest*, *Spirit & Destiny*, and *Llewellyn's Magical Almanac*. She has appeared on morning shows on both Fox and NBC, and her feng shui work was featured on the Bravo TV show *Flipping Out*.

Tess's teachings about magic and spirituality appear extensively online, particularly on her website, TessWhitehurst.com, and via her online membership portal, Wisdom Circle Online School of Magical Arts.

Tess lives in the Central Valley of California with a handsome man and a handsome cat.

Visit Tess and sign up for her free newsletter at **TessWhitehurst.com**

About the Artist

TAMMY WAMPLER is an artist and author of *The Maidens of the Wheel* oracle deck. The path to becoming an artist was like the ever-turning spiral for Tammy. She worked as an archaeologist, a massage and reiki practitioner, and a tarot and past-life reader, before focusing on her art full-time. Tammy draws on her deep understanding of myth and history as well as her intuitive knowledge of symbolism and culture in the creation of her works.

Found in public and private collections and exhibited worldwide, Tammy's artworks concentrate on the figurative and are expressed in oils, acrylics, and soft pastels. Her creations are influenced by Magic Realism, Art Nouveau, and Fantasy and convey a strong sense of emotion through the eyes of her subjects. Tammy's exploration of strength and vulnerability is woven with shamanism, mysticism, and myth to portray engaging feminine archetypes.

Tammy lives in the beautiful Bluegrass Region of Kentucky, USA, with her family and three cats. Discover more of her work at **www.tammywampler.artweb.com**

Also available from Blue Angel Publishing®

THE ORACLE OF DAYDREAMS & MOONBEAMS
Wisdom and Guidance from Fairytales, Fantasy, and Folklore

Tess Whitehurst
Artwork by Jessica von Braun

Within these cards lies a tapestry of magic and metaphor inspired by fables, fantasy, and folklore, ready to guide you toward joy and fulfillment.

Like silver slippers and a treasure map, this 46-card oracle deck and guidebook illuminate the yellow brick road to living fully, bravely, and happily. Each card offers you wisdom and whimsy to navigate life's twists and turns while embracing every precious moment.

As you embark on your personal hero's journey, remember that true transformation lies in the quest itself, not just the destination. Whether outsmarting witches, saving kingdoms, or seeking grails, let this oracle be your companion, supporting you through rainstorms, lost mittens, and uphill climbs — to your own happily-ever-after.

ISBN: 978-1-922574-24-4
46 cards and 128-page guidebook.

Also available from Blue Angel Publishing®

THE ANGEL MAGIC ORACLE
Empowering Guidance & Divine Love

Tess Whitehurst
Artwork by Jessica von Braun

Angel magic is accessible to all who seek it. In this ethereal oracle, you have a direct link to the boundless support, insight, and blessings of the celestial realms. Hold the deck to your heart to align yourself with the luminous presence of the angels. Welcome their energy as you shuffle and choose your cards. The big questions and the small ones are received by the angels with love, so you always receive wise, relevant, and practical responses in accord with your highest healing, purpose, and possibility.

ISBN: 978-1-922573-93-3
56 cards and 144-page guidebook.

Also available from Blue Angel Publishing®

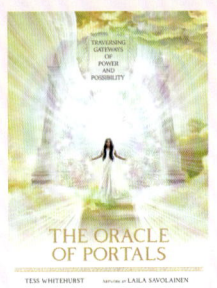

THE ORACLE OF PORTALS
Traversing Gateways of Power and Possibility

Tess Whitehurst
Artwork by Laila Savolainen

Between what is and what may be are realms of possibility.
Open magical doors, step through,
and behold the dreams that call to you.

Come beyond the bounds of time and place to discover the profound and transformative power of the in-between. You are forever on the threshold of becoming, and every turn, choice, action, and word is a path maker. Now, you can consciously navigate the liminal to open the gateways to your brighter future.

Journey through and explore the portals of this beautifully illustrated 44-card set, and let your pathway unfold as a glorious expression of your magical self. Be bold, be true — your tomorrow awaits!

ISBN: 978-1-922573-43-8
44 cards and 148-page guidebook.

Also available from Blue Angel Publishing®

MAIDENS OF THE WHEEL ORACLE CARDS
Inner Journeys through the Cycles of the Year

Tammy Wampler

The Maidens of the Wheel have been known in many places and by many names throughout history. They dance through the cosmos, embodying inspiration and whispering guidance. They are here to empower and align you with sacred rhythms and lost traditions. Work with these elemental beings to discover harmony within the cycles of your life and embrace your true, unshakable center.

"When we are unaware of the energies and cycles at play, they can feel chaotic. By reorienting with them, they can become inspiring, empowering, grounding, and profoundly healing. The loving strength of Goddess Earth will open you to connection, realization, direction, and manifestation as never before." — Tammy Wampler

ISBN: 978-1-922573-90-2
45 cards and 120-page guidebook.

For more information on this
or any Blue Angel Publishing® release,
please visit our website at:

www.blueangelonline.com